TRUE RAPE CASE STORIES

16 NARRATIONS AND ENCOUNTERS OF TRUE RAPE CASES, SEXUAL ABUSE AND SURVIVAL

KAREN J. BENNETT

D1522671

TABLE OF CONTENTS

CHAPTER ONE

INTRODUCTION

Stories of rape victims may be extremely taxing, terrifying, and difficult to read for some, but they also serve to remind other victims that they are not alone in their suffering. Rape narratives describe the many traumas that some individuals experience but manage to endure and go on to heal from and reclaim control of their life. People may learn from the experiences of other rape survivors and know that they are not alone in going through what they have and coming out the other side whole.

The following rape narratives include abuse, sexual assault, incest, and violent incidents. Even though the individuals in these rape victim tales have been severely hurt by these incidents, they still have the fortitude to speak up about what has happened to them. Each of these rape-related tales demonstrates the bravery of the survivor.

Rape is typically committed by family members: uncles, aunts, fathers, nephews, teachers, and domestic employees. The majority of males were assaulted by aunties and madams - people you can trust.

Statistics show that just 7% of abusers are strangers. Sixty-three percent are family members, while thirty percent are close acquaintances. Threat is their most powerful tool.

And talking about it is the first step toward healing. Sharing the story with someone who has gone through the same thing may be reassuring since they understand.

So we think you can recover and start doing wonderful things. Oprah Winfrey and Joyce Meyer are two of our favorite role models.

Oprah Winfrey was raped by her uncle and became pregnant, but the child died. She is now the wealthiest black lady on the planet.

Joyce Meyer was raped serially as a kid by her father, yet she is now one of the world's finest preachers. So our purpose is to heal since most women who are emotionally wounded are unable to have excellent children.

In this volume you will read about a young girl who was abused sexually by her father, a neighbor and a preacher. Her mother was present, but there was nothing she could do about it.

You will find a story of another young girl was forcefully persuaded by her boyfriend to sleep with his friends else she will be left in the middle of the woods with no one to help her and they took turns on her.

Then there is a story of another teenager whose vodka was drugged by her friend and she didn't know has been raped until she got home and found bruises on her.

As you read further, you will come across a young girl named Kris, Just few days before Christmas; her parents have gone for a Christmas get together at a friend's place. Kris, was left at home all by herself, her rapist had been in the building long before her parents left. After watching them for a couple of days, she was just a teenager. She was abused repeatedly for two hours at different parts of the house as she tries to escape. "You are No 10" she told him before he left.

Every story in this book necessitates hours of investigations. Newspaper, articles, police reports, and firsthand accounts from victims. As unpleasant and emotionally taxing as rape stories might be for some to read, the objective of this book is not to terrify or disturb anybody, but to inform you on the events and heighten your awareness and security procedure.

These stories come from all around the world and have no common link, yet they are both thought simulating, scary, and will leave you with a fresh perspective on how fragile the human mind can be.

Lastly, for reasons known to the author, the names of the victims have been left out while some have been altered to fit in into the narration.

It concludes with a chapter on rape recovery and rehabilitation. It further explains the healing process, how to cope with sexual abuse and what to do as a rape victim or to help a rape victim. All suggestions were derived from real life experiences that have proved effective for the victims whose stories have been told in this text.

True Rape Stories

CHAPTER TWO

THE UNTOLD STORIES

1. FOR SIX YEARS, I COULDN'T SPEAK UP – I WAS JUST A TEEN

My nightmare started when I was 12 years old.

My parents sent me to be with my uncle since they couldn't afford to train us all.

Of course, I was overjoyed to be moving out of town, but that happiness was to become sour and stay so throughout my teenage years.

The first night (shortly after I arrived), it may have been a dream, only I was certain it was real.

A hand groped m9y body, first touching my nipples and then my vagina.

I was terrified since it was dark and I couldn't figure out who might be doing this to me. And since I grew up in a strict Christian environment where sex was never discussed, the idea of someone touching my genital organs was strange to me.

In fact, my initial reaction was disbelief that someone could touch my genital.

That night passed, and the hand continued to come every night until he eventually entered me after approximately a week.

Still, I assumed it was a monster until my uncle walked over and threatened me, saying, 'If you ever tell anybody what is going on in this home, I will kill you.'

I never imagined it could have been him, despite the fact that he was my favorite uncle and I adored him. He apparently assumed I was aware.

He also said that my mother, who is a devout Christian, would never trust me. And I trusted him. It was a very unbelievable tale.

Naturally, I bled the first time, but his wife mistook it for my period and offered me a sanitary pad. Even today, I can't explain how his wife never found out, despite the fact that we all shared a one-room apartment and they slept in the same bed.

I honestly don't know whether she knew or guessed but didn't say anything. So many things occurred back then that I still don't understand, like never becoming pregnant.

Anyway, after deflowering me, he began having intercourse with me on a daily basis, and I honestly can't count how many times he raped me.

I became his other sex choice, and it lasted six years - on and off - until I was 18. I was OK when he wasn't around, but I wasn't fine when he was.

I thought I had done something wrong after that initial penetration and regretted myself. As a Christian girl, my mother had taught me that being a virgin was the finest gift I could offer my spouse, so I felt robbed of a treasure. I felt completely worthless and useless.

He obviously preyed on my gullibility since informing anybody never occurred to me. I had no idea about sexual abuse or that I could file a complaint against him.

My religious upbringing kept me innocent. Our life centered around church, and we seldom spoke to anybody who were not members of our church.

My father, despite being a military guy, was a zonal coordinator before he died, and my mother is now the head of a local assembly. In fact, I assumed this was occurring to me because God despised me.

"I was the eldest and grew breasts at a young age. Aside than that, I'm not sure why he chose me. I was disappointed since this was someone I called 'dad'.

That notion almost killed me. Nonetheless, I refused to forgive myself. I assumed he selected me because I bore an awful mark. I had the impression that God disliked me.

Why did my parents choose me to live away from them? Why did they have me when they knew they couldn't care for me? For a long period, I carried that remorse and humiliation.

I imagined it would have been more difficult for him if I had been wearing slacks instead of long dresses. As a result, I now wear pants and my girls do not wear skirts.

My kid was supposed to attend a school where everyone wore skirts. I wouldn't let her leave for that reason alone.

That event ruined my life. I was taken to a psychiatric hospital due to mental disorders. For years, I struggled with depression and was on antidepressants.

My kid is 15 years old, and I've been hypertensive for the same amount of time. Every day, I take blood pressure medicine.

I wish my spouse would agree to share his experience so you could understand how this has affected me. You should start speaking with males who are married to women who have been sexually assaulted or raped.

It gets in the way of your relationship with your spouse. By the way, I married to get away from my uncle's place, not necessarily because I was in love.

Yes, the rape went on, and there was nowhere to go. He never let me speak to any male. My mother, who was 37 at the time, already had nine children, so moving in with her was out of the question.

To add insult to injury, and make matters worse, my father died. Things went on like this until I met a preacher.

My friend had invited me to a new church on our block. When the preacher said, 'If you want to devote your life to Christ, please come forward,' I walked out because I believed what my uncle was doing to me was wrong and that God despised me.

Things would change if I devoted my life to Christ, I reasoned. After the service, the preacher wanted to talk with the new converts, and then he asked to speak with me alone.

Meanwhile, I didn't know him and had never met him, but he stated I had something to speak to him, which surprised me.

I said, 'No,' to which he replied, 'You want to tell me that your uncle is sexually assaulting you and you don't know what to do.'

I immediately knelt down and began weeping. He let me weep for a bit before handing me a handkerchief to wipe my tears. He said that my uncle would return that night and then asked, 'Do you want this to stop?' 'Yes,' I said. I was 18.

I couldn't tell his wife since I didn't know I could. It may be tough to believe, yet that is how a child's mind operates.

That early danger stayed with me throughout my childhood and teen years. Even when I sent letters to my mother, he was the one who delivered them to the post office and would always urge me, 'Make

18

sure you don't mention anything about what's going on in this home in that letter.'

He also made certain that I arrived home from school on time. And I was not about to disregard such threats. My uncle was 6 feet tall.

Furthermore, as a Christian girl, you don't want anybody to know that such harm was done to you.

It's very simple to argue that I remained silent because I was getting into it, but I never did. Even after 17 years of marriage, I still don't like sex.

I could go fourteen weeks without having sex with my spouse, despite the fact that we sleep in the same bed. Sexual abuse affects you in one of two ways: you get addicted to sex or you lose interest in sex entirely.

So everyone who claims that I remained silent because I was having fun is mistaken. What are you having fun with? Sex that was violently presented to you!

As a kid! By your very own uncle! There's nothing there to appreciate. I have no desire for sex. My good fortune is that I am married to a guy who loves and cherishes me; who has brought me to a psychiatric hospital and never used it against me.

I asked my spouse not to have sex with me the day we married because I was experiencing triggers. I also instructed him not to lie nude alongside me and not to say 'I love you,' call me 'Darling, Dear,' or use any other terms of affection that my uncle was using on me. So now my hubby just addresses me by my first name.

So, when people say things like, 'She's loving it,' I simply tell them it's because I'm not their daughter; if I was, they'd be sympathetic. I was 12, for crying out loud! "I had no idea about sex!"

"Until 12 years into my marriage, I couldn't sleep nude near my spouse. It's so severe that my husband needs to be with me throughout labor because I can't be alone in a room with another guy or I'll have panic attacks.

He would have to be there if I had to visit a male doctor throughout my pregnancy. I acquired a fear of males. I've told him I was leaving multiple times.

But he's a kind guy, and I'm still in the marriage due to his efforts. He knows how much I've gone through. He is there for me when I am having tantrums and experiencing acute depression.

After three children, I entered myself into a mental health facility without informing my family because I was growing psychotic and hearing voices instructing me to commit myself.

The encounter made me feel insignificant. I had purchased pills on several times in order to commit suicide. 'I'm not good enough for you,' I'd tell my spouse. Don't worry, when I die, the church will provide you with a better wife.'

My uncle was never seen again. He phoned a year ago to apologize.

That was his first experience. I believe he came to apologize because I had begun publicly criticizing him. He apologized profusely and asked that I please forgive him.

My whole family gathered; my mother, my siblings; they'd all begged me to let go. My mother advised me to stop talking about it publicly, but it has now gone beyond me since I lead a support group for women recuperating from rape and abuse.

I no longer mention my uncle's name since I'm not out to harm him. I tell my tale not because I'm in pain, but to inspire other victims to unburden and recover.

My schooling was also severely harmed as a result of the incident. I was doing part-time but had to quit in Year 2 due to my trauma.

Worse, I had no idea I could seek professional assistance or counseling. By the time I realized, it was too late, and I had to settle with taking classes to teach myself.

Sexual assault deprives you of your life's significance. My children were terrified every time I wanted to go out and would say, 'Mummy, hope you're not attempting to run away again?' since I once did.

I told you I once checked into a psychiatric institution; I didn't tell them, I didn't tell my husband, and I refused to give the hospital his phone number.

Even the hospital was concerned about being sued. I purposefully left my phone at home and erased the last calls so they couldn't track me down."

'My experiences almost turned me into a nympho,'

2. ALL I WANTED WAS TO SEE THE AQUARIUM

I was eager to see the aquarium.

Jimmy was the first person to ever see my naked chest.

We were both 12 at the time.

After I repeatedly refused, he pushed my shirt up so he could view my chest. It began as a lighthearted kiss. I chuckled and went off.

Jimmy was the son of my dad's closest buddy.

Parents who are close friends force their children to socialize.

Despite the distance between us and them, we used to go there throughout the summer to attend big family get-togethers.

The first time I met Colin, Jimmy's cousin, was at a party. Colin was 18 and I was 14.

Colin was the first person to ever give me a drink. He handed me a drink as we stood in the side yard with many children. My younger brother was around when I said no, and I'm too independent to give in to peer pressure. Years went by. Colin would ask when I was going back to visit again, like and remark on my Instagram photos, contact me on my birthday, and do other pretty harmless things.

I enjoyed the focus.

With the independence of college and some money in my pocket, I was feeling daring as a sophomore in college. Since it was the biggest aquarium in the nation, I informed Colin that I would want to visit. I purchased a ticket. He got us passes to the aquarium. Colin was 23 and I was 19.

I assumed everything would be well since he was a family friend. My dad planned lunch with Colin's uncle so I could meet him while I was there since he knew I would be there. We spent a really laid-back day and a half visiting the aquarium, sightseeing, and tasting different foods after Colin picked me up from the airport. He warned me to stop messaging my friends and focus on what was going on with him every time I picked up my phone.

He offered that I share the bed with him when it was time to go to sleep. On both nights, I declined the offer and slept on the floor. I changed into all my clothing in the bathroom before taking a shower so I wouldn't have to go outside in a towel. I didn't pack any flirtatious attire. We went to hang out with both his male and female college mates. We played Frisbee, watched football, ate Chinese cuisine, and decided at the last minute to see Andy Grammar and O.A.R. I declined Colin's offer to pay for my ticket and did it myself. I used my fictitious identification to purchase a Blue Moon when I was seated at the rooftop bar above the performance site.

It was so cool.

Colin asked the gang to remain with him for one more drink before they all headed down to the show. He sat across from me and said that if I lived close enough, he would date me right away. I friend-zoned him after rejecting that idea.

Apparently, he handled it nicely. The group we came with was waiting for us when we went downstairs.

Andy Grammar performed his whole performance. O.A.R. performed their whole set. I was photographed by Andy Grammar (I only know because I have the photos).

Using my phony ID, we departed and proceeded to four other bars. I'm not sure how I got in. Nothing comes to mind.

Colin dropped me out at the airport the next morning. After passing through security, I went to the restroom, and when I urinated, it stung. Did we have sex? I texted Colin; Yes, he replied. I was very perplexed. I drove back to college after flying home, telling my father it had been a terrific vacation. I had only spent a few hours at college when I suddenly had swelling in my hands and feet, along with hives. I had a steroid injection at MedExpress.

It did not assist. After taking additional allergy medication and steroids that evening, my hands swelled so much that I was unable to sign my release paperwork at the ER. Days went by. I caught a little moment of awareness returning. Colin was standing above me as I lay on a futon, squeezing into me. I stood up, gathered my pants, and entered the restroom.

Was it a dream or did it really happen?

A few days or weeks later, I was at the mall when I heard an O.A.R. song, which caused me to start crying and force myself to leave. I had no idea why. The weeks that followed saw me begin to drink a lot. I often became unconscious. But no blackout compared to the one with Colin that night. I began to understand that the night I spent with Colin wasn't a typical blackout.

I searched up the side effects of medications used in dating rape. I had ample time to return to college without experiencing a response since the GHB reaction might take up to 24-48 hours to manifest.

About two months after the trip, I came to terms with Colin having drugged and raped me. I told my dad while spending the weekend at home.

He came over and gave me a bear embrace after punching the kitchen counter.

My father raged and summoned his buddy. Colin's father contacted my father and threatened to put Colin on a plane unless he came up to apologize to me.

I refused. I never desired to see them once again. My father steadfastly refused to go there, not even for business.

Colin taught me how to eat pho, so I didn't for years. When I see a Mazda Miata, I wince.

Even though I don't recall hearing it, there is some music from that weekend that I can't listen to.

I was allergic to the painkiller fentanyl when I had my wisdom teeth removed at the age of 23. Allergies to GHB and fentanyl are related. Five years or so have passed. I still live with it every day.

I still question myself.

3. GANGED RAPED AT 17

I went to a pop concert against my parents' wishes in October 1985. By the end of the night, I'd been gang raped in identical conditions to the 17-year-old girl who accused numerous guys, including Premiership players, of raping her at the Grosvenor House hotel. The guys who assaulted me were neither superstars nor even wealthy. They were, in actuality, nobody. But, they were beauty personified to me, a 14-year-old girl who was only 4ft 11in tall and had very little experience in the world.

The guys, who were six years my senior were in a pop band that played in clubs and sometimes supported larger acts. They spoke about a glossy world of recording studios and record contracts that I was unfamiliar with. Their expressions pouted out of photos in the local paper. They were well-known in their community. They were a group with catchphrases I didn't understand, primarily about sex activities, and small hand gestures that my closest buddy and I imitated and laughed about on the playground at lunchtime.

That night, I looked up at them from the stage, and when they smiled, pointed me out, and waved, I felt grown-up, gorgeous, and significant. I'd been seeing Liam for three weeks and had met Phil and Simon once or twice. Liam requested that I remain out the night of the event. He recommended I lie to my parents and claim I was at a girlfriend's place, so we could "spend the entire night together". I would have done everything he asked because I had fallen in love with this guy who talked of grown-up things and said, "I can't believe you're only 14, you seem so much older" - although the images I now look at show that I didn't. When I initially met him, he said he couldn't believe I was a virgin. He couldn't believe his good fortune.

So I made an excuse and went to the show. I wasn't offered champagne, but rather a cheap vodka. I didn't drink much of it and wasn't even inebriated. I was never a heavy drinker as a teenager. The lads were on a high after the performance, enjoying the attention of their groupies. I waited for half an hour as they circulated before they came up to me. Liam inquired as to whether I had made plans to remain out. I answered sure, and he hurriedly hustled me out the door, followed by the others.

Liam asked whether I wanted to remain at Simon's place where we could "all be together" or go back to the bedsit of the band's fourth member. (He was a model and actor who was attending a party.) I couldn't figure out what the underlying message was. I assumed he intended us to spend the night alone together at Simon's, so I went with that option. He then informed me that he took this as my permission. The fact that you asked me where I wanted to stay was interpreted as permission to group sex.

Our county had been terrorized the previous year by a rapist known as the Fox. Malcolm Fairley broke into residences at night and raped women in front of their spouses at gunpoint. My father would remain up all night after barricading the windows to protect his family. He was certain that no rapist would get near us.

With my father looking over me, I felt safe. Rape, I believed, was a guy climbing through your window in the middle of the night. After days of begging and pleading with my parents, I never imagined it would happen at a small music festival, my first ever. I didn't expect Liam to spend three weeks getting to know me before introducing me to his buddies.

I was shown to a little contemporary residence. There was a black leather couch, black ash veneer furniture, and semi-naked ladies' images by Athena. I assume it was a bachelor pad from the 1980s, but I'd never been in one before. I still had a Pierrot duvet cover on my bed. The guys stated they were exhausted and suggested we go to bed. Liam led the way up the steps, and I followed. I was perplexed as we entered the room. I asked Liam where we were going to sleep. "We'll all cram in together," he added.

As the other guys went to bed, I asked Liam if we could sleep downstairs, but Phil became angry and instructed us to hurry up since he needed to sleep, and Liam leaped at his instruction, urging me along. Still with my shirt and underwear on, I climbed into bed next to the guy I had trusted, knowing I wouldn't sleep a wink.

The light went out, and Liam began to touch me. I responded, no, that it wasn't right with his buddies present, and wanted to go downstairs again. But he wasn't even paying attention. He slept with me. I won't call it rape, though it was statutory rape due to my age, but I was uncomfortable and uncooperative, loathing every minute of it. I figured if I simply let him do it, it would be done and I'd be able to wait out the long hours until it was safe to return home without raising my parents' suspicions. Then the light turned on, and Phil said, "Can we join in?" "Be my guest," Liam replied. None of them asked me.

I'm not going to torment the reader or myself with specifics of what they did to me. To put it simply, I was the victim of a "ramming," one of their catchphrases. Simon and Phil raped me in turn, each with the "help" of the other. I can still feel the cold metal of Phil's nipple-rings rubbing against my body as I was ripped apart in every way. I often awaken from dreams in which my air is being squeezed out of me, a tremendous weight is pressing down on me, and the fragrance of his cologne fills my nostrils.

I "stayed for breakfast" like the 17-year-old female, albeit I didn't eat anything. I waited for them to take me home as I watched them load their faces with fried egg sandwiches. I couldn't contact my parents or go home early because they'd find out I'd lied, and I was terrified, as many teens are. So I sat and waited for them to drive me home. I ran a hot bath and started a year-long practice of scouring my body in an effort to clean it. Friends regularly make fun of my obsessive-compulsive cleaning habits, but the root of my preoccupation rests in that night.

For the last 18 years, I have lived with the guilt and repercussions of their acts. The emotional fallout has been massive. I tried suicide soon after the incident, but I never told a person about it. The males, on the other hand, boasted about the "three's up," as they phrased it. However, it was not considered rape. It was perceived that I was a slag, an eager participant in group sex even though I was a youngster with no experience with guys like them and practically no experience with sex. Since then, I've been plagued by severe depression, panic attacks, nightmares, and other symptoms of post-traumatic stress disorder.

The physical effects of that night left me scarred, and the bodily harm I experienced during the assault has had major health ramifications for me ever since.

Other than the unending love of my spouse and family, I have suffered with my filthy secret without any form of treatment or assistance. But now, wherever I look, there's a story about a young girl who claims she was gang raped by a bunch of guys who wooed her with their notoriety. It's in every newspaper, on the radio, and TV. It's not hearing about it in the media that makes me angry, but rather the comments and opinions of others who question what she was doing drinking in those kinds of bars, pursuing those kinds of men, returning to hotel rooms with strangers, and in their judgment of her behavior, I feel judged - even though they have no idea what happened to me.

I admire the courage of any teenager who tells her parents or goes to the police. Much of my rage is directed at myself for being unable to achieve these things. I could only perceive it as my fault when I was 14 years old. I lied to my parents, consented to go the said cabin, didn't know how to stop the guys from raping me, and couldn't face my family with so much humiliation. I didn't report the rape for many years, and even then, I concluded I couldn't go through with it. I'd moved away, hoping to forget what had occurred.

Liam showed up for an event in my state of residence16 years later. I had him thrown out. Phil subsequently showed up at a friend's party only a few minutes away from my house. He greeted me as though we were old friends. I confronted him with the truth, furious.

"The point is, Emilia, we truly liked you," he said. We considered you a member of the group."

But I was never a member of their group. Their group was all about humiliating and demeaning sexual actions on schoolgirls. The terrifying aspect is that this has always occurred. It occurs in small towns and cities throughout the nation, as well as on municipal estates and in middle-class suburbs. It occurs to lovely females and girls who get intoxicated in pubs and clubs, and it will continue to happen until this problem is addressed.

I don't think Phil or Simon realized they were committing rape at the moment. This form of intercourse was considered "normal" by them. Liam subsequently informed me that he assumed I was taking part. "You never said anything," he pointed out. When presented with the victim's point of view, they are compelled to reconsider their behavior totally. I asked Phil to envision his 14-year-old daughter in the same circumstances as mine. Is this considered rape? I wanted him to see me as a human, a kid, not a piece of meat. "Looking at that circumstance [the rape], I can probably paint it blacker in my brain than you can," he continued. I don't think so, but I do feel he is now aware that rape involves more than simply seizing a lady at knifepoint in a dark alleyway.

Young males must be educated that rape does not occur simply when a female cries, yells, and kicks. There are several sorts of authority, and a woman does not always need to be restrained. I didn't yell, scream, or kick. I laid with my eyes closed, sobbing quietly, while Phil grabbed Simon by the hips and forced him into me, screaming "Ram, ram, ram" and laughing. He then inquired as to whether I had cum.

4. ABUSED SEXUALLY SERIALLY FOR THE NEXT TWO HOURS

Kris, 15, was playing the piano in the living room by herself when she heard the gentle sound of cloth unraveling. She took a breather. It's nothing, she reasoned. She continued her game.

A huge guy appeared behind her, placing a knife to her neck. She reasoned that if she coughed, it would enter her body.

"If you move, I'll murder you," he rasped between his clinched teeth. As he put prepared restraints — her sister's shoelaces — around her wrists, she complied in mind-numbing horror. He shoved a handkerchief from his pocket into her mouth as a gag, then forced her to the outdoor picnic table.

"If you say anything or flinch," he said, "I'll shove the knife all the way in and disappear in the middle of the night."

It was a few days before Christmas, and the first in a series of progressively terrifying assaults on scared suburbanites in Sacramento and elsewhere. The rapist would go from sneak attacks on susceptible victims to all-out assaults on couples and whole families in the residence. He would imprison men with plates balanced on their backs while their wives were raped repeatedly. He kept the kids in the bathroom. He lingered, rifled drawers and ransacked the kitchen, and gazed calmly at his victims for extended periods of time.

He'd been following them for days, standing outside windows and in the bushes. He sneaked through police patrols unnoticed, planting false clues to mock investigators.

Kris had only been at home for 10 minutes. Her parents had gone to a Christmas party. Her sister was working. Her closest buddy had just returned from baking Christmas cookies. Later, she'd assume he'd been waiting inside the closet all along.

The guy in the red ski mask pulled the adolescent outdoors and back in, dragging her from room to room to rape and attack her repeatedly over the next two hours. He inserted his penis between her chained hands behind her back and told her to touch it — a practice repeated so often in his assaults that police began to depend on forced masturbation as an identifying attribute. Then he raped her on her parents' bed, three times in the living room, and once in front of the fireplace.

"Isn't this great?" He spoke into her ear.

He sent the tied, nude girl back outside into the cold to shiver while he rifled through the home, returning to the same spots again and over. In the buffet, she heard the clinking of silverware.

She put him to the test by shifting her elbow. He was immediately on her, his rough voice in her ear.

Kris moved again after the third rape, when she believed she couldn't take it any longer, and found he was gone.

This was her introduction to a shadowy sisterhood of 49 rape and sexual assault survivors who were so nameless to the rest of the world that when they met 40 years later, they identified themselves by number. "Hello, I'm No. 10," Kris would say.

5. MY "NO" WASN'T POWERFUL ENOUGH - I FELT USED SO I BEGAN OFFERING MYSELF OUT

My sexual molestation and rape history extends back to my childhood, when I was repeatedly assaulted.

In actuality, there were around five occurrences. It began with my home lesson instructor, who would put his hands beneath the table and touch my laps and private parts even though my siblings were around. Of course, they didn't see or notice anything.

I was in second or third grade and assumed it was just one of those things that everyone goes through.

Even then, I knew it wasn't normal since I had attempted suicide as a youngster in elementary school.

Nobody was at home one day, so I quickly packed some medications and consumed them. I couldn't get away from the molestations since the instructor always showed there.

He tutored me in French for over four years. Despite the fact that he merely used his fingers, I always felt unclean.

So I'd spend my time in the bathroom washing and sobbing. I was irritated because no matter how hard I tried, I couldn't get it off.

Mum most likely felt something was wrong and continued asking, but I couldn't tell her. I couldn't tell my older sister, who was equally little, although six years older.

She thought I had problems. When I finally opened up to tell my mother, she told me it was my fault. That ruined my friendship with her.

I used to despise her, but we've reconciled. I also despised myself: I despised my skin color, I despised my looks; I believed I drew these things to myself.

When I confided in my elementary school friends, they were taken aback. That was a revelation to me.

The irony is that pedophiles are pedophiles regardless of whether a kid is fair or beautiful. They are just drawn to children. And they keep an eye out for the weakest link.

Now that I'm a psychologist, I know better. I know it wasn't my fault. I can't even remember what the instructor looked like since it's been a long time, but the harm was done.

I grew up with a victim mentality, which, according to experts, attracts such things. It's the same way that women in toxic situations attract abusers."

"When I was 17, a buddy raped me. He was 23 years old and was like a closest friend to me since I grew up to be a tomboy. All of my buddies were guys; I had no idea I'd wind up married with three children.

We were conversing indoors, which wasn't uncommon, when he began making attempts toward me. I complained, but I wasn't as forceful. That again, is what poor self-esteem does to individuals.

My **'NO'** wasn't powerful enough, so by the time he began pushing me, I had frozen - in the same way that some people freeze in the face of danger.

So it's not like he assaulted me. Long story short, he got his way and humiliated me in the process, but the entire thing was strange for me since I fought till the very end and sobbed afterwards.

In fact, I immediately proceeded to get a knife and try to murder myself, and then he began pleading and expressing regret. However, the harm had already been done. It was psychological in nature."

"That incident is one of the reasons I now work as a counseling psychologist, educating young women to be more aggressive.

Even when females say 'no,' it is a sign of weakness, and men tend to take it for granted. Make it plain in your body language that you are not in favor of it. A woman who exudes enough self-assurance sends a clear message.

In any case, it occurred again. You might argue that my previous experiences should have taught me not to approach guys too closely, but I was an incurable optimist.

However, such incidents shattered my trust in humans. I'm still working on regaining trust in individuals as we speak.

I was 24 at the time and had recently lost my father. We were having so many guests who had come to express their condolences to us that I decided to take a break.

I ended up going to a friend's house - as I previously said, my buddies are all male. It wasn't too late, approximately 1800hours, so I believed I'd be home by 1900hours.

He began making advances, and I politely declined. But, since the door was shut, I began racing around the room, attempting to get away from him.

But he persisted, and eventually he came to perceive it as a game, which made it much more irritating. And he continued saying to me, 'After all, you stated you're not a virgin,' as if it was an excuse.

When I think about it, I want to escape that chapter of my life, but I also want to assist other females by sharing my experience. Looking back, there are several things I should have done differently."

He eventually came up with me, restrained me, and had his way. I returned home, had a bath, and went to bed. Of course, no one else was aware.

But then I started a new era of my life and began having   series of relationships. It wasn't a man-a-day thing, and I wasn't sleeping with guys for money - I always believed I was worth more than that - but I went into various situations where I gladly offered myself.

Instead of guys pressuring me, I said, let me take command, take liberty, and enjoy it. Of course, sex is sex, and it's not always a negative thing.

I'd even make the first move on some occasions. It lasted approximately a year; I was in my twenties and in college at the time. I even thought I was a nymphomaniac at one time. Fortunately, I had several pals who could assist me.

"As a consequence, I've had difficulties. I used to have recurring dreams of getting raped. My spouse is alert, so when I scream in the middle of the night, he is attentive.

It's better now, and I'm having less flashbacks. Our marriage has lasted seven years.

Most of the time, what we dream about are the things we're scared of, since our brain is free to roam at that time.

So now I'm always on the lookout for my three children (two girls and a boy). I'm always chatting with them and asking them questions, and I hardly allow them out of my sight. At the same time, one should avoid becoming paranoid.

I'm also starting to realize that the trauma never goes away. Sometimes we believe we have completely recovered, but it leaves scars that are deeper than we realize.

Aside from trust, I've noticed that I still struggle with poor self-esteem on occasion.

That's why I joined a support group: to speak about it with other women who have gone through similar experiences. As a result, it takes time to recover.

I also give thanks to God for my marriage. My spouse is completely understanding. I made it a point to tell him everything about my background before committing to a serious relationship with him.

I told him I didn't want a situation where he would come across anything and say, 'I don't want a damaged product.' He chuckled about it, but it helped us form a close bond."

CHAPTER THREE

SHATTERING THE SILENCE

6. AFTER MULTIPLE NOS'; STILL NOT BELIEVED BY THE COURT

At the age of ten, I was abused by a local bully for the first time. Then, between the ages of 14 and 27, I was sexually abused by a family member. I was raped in my late 30s by someone I was sleeping with. I'm not proud of it, but he wanted his friend to touch me, and I refused. I wanted nothing at that time. When his buddy left, he began caressing me and I told him, no, but he wouldn't stop, and I froze.

Someone else raped me again last year. I'd already said no. I didn't want anything more from him, but he still came over and raped me. He trapped me against my bedroom wall as I continued saying no. He was much more powerful than I was. He shut my bedroom door and refused to let me go. I told him I didn't want to be wounded, but he wouldn't listen.

He then shoved me back to the bed and pinned me down, and I continued saying no. I told him to get to his girlfriend, who was the person with whom he was living with. He seemed not to hear or care about what I was saying. He continued to rape me despite my repeated refusals. I eventually froze. I didn't weep, and I didn't do anything. He nearly choked me, but he stopped when he noticed I was struggling to breathe. He even apologized for almost strangling me. He began yanking my shorts off. I was ready for it to be done. I didn't want him around. It was over in a flash.

Following that, he behaved as if nothing had occurred, and it felt as if nothing had happened. It began running through my thoughts after he went, and I still don't want to think about it. Even though

I knew NO meant NO, I felt like I deserved it since I didn't love him.

He didn't give a damn about me. I suppose that was the only way to make me know he was callous and that I needed to keep him away. Nothing was done. I filed charges, but the detectives didn't believe me since I had previously slept with him, so there's nothing more I can do except attempt to heal myself from my upbringing.

Even though I know the reality, I continue to blame myself. I'm afraid I'll never be believed again. I can't trust anybody, but I'm holding out hope because I need to take care of my kid. One day, it will all be over. I will live a better life, and my history will no longer have the same impact on me as it does today.

I may not trust anybody right now since I am terrified of getting close to anyone. I have so many triggers and fears, but one day they will all be forgotten. Because of the embarrassment, I'm not sure I'll be able to convey the whole tale of what occurred last year. A part of me is still processing what occurred. I just knew that I said no multiple times and he wouldn't let me go. I wasn't intimidated or beaten, but he wouldn't let me go.

I was terrified and ashamed when I had to speak in front of a crowd in court. I felt unbelieved, I guess I must have earned it. It didn't seem to matter what I thought. I'm undergoing extensive counseling for suicidal ideation. How could I think that way when I have my kid and, thus I must survive. I'm not going to let them triumph, and I'm not going to remain quiet.

NO, NO, NO!!! That was not fair to me.

7. HE WAS A FIRST A FRIEND, THEN BECAME A WOLF – MY WORST NIGHTMARE

This occurred to me when I was 19 years old. I was watching a movie at my buddy Mike's place. He leaned in and kissed me as I was watching the movie.

I was at a loss for words and kissed him back. He attempted to kiss me again, but I declined, telling him I was just there to see the movie. "Oh, please!, "I know you want it," he added as he kissed me harder. I continued pleading with him to stop. Then he began "passionately" kissing me and stroking my private areas under my clothing.

Before I could protest at him, he was on top of me, pinning me down and ripping my clothing off. "Don't worry, I know how to do a female correctly," he stated as he undressed. I attempted to flee out the door when he wasn't on top of me, even though I was half-naked.

"What the hell, Katherine?" he said as he seized my shoulders. I thought you loved me? "Didn't you kiss me back?" Then he tossed me onto the sofa. He slapped me across the face and placed his hands around my neck. He jumped back on top of me, grabbed my mouth with his other hand, and began to finger me. He informed me that I "loved what he was doing" or that I was "enjoying it" every time I shouted. Then he sexually assaulted me (forcible sexual intercourse).

When he was through, he spits on my face and changed his clothes. He called me a "dirty little whore" as he left me in the fetal position, weeping. I hurriedly put my clothes back on after he had been gone for a few minutes. I rushed out of there as quickly and fast as I could.

After that, I never spoke to him again. I drove myself home and took a really hot shower to attempt to get him off of me. I didn't go to the hospital because I was afraid he'd come after me and rape me again.

I did notify the bishop of my church about it and the bishop asked me a series of sexual questions, perhaps to find out whether it was "truly a rape case".

He continued asking me questions like,

"Did you get wet?"

"Have you been sexually aroused?"

"Can you tell me what you were wearing?"

"Did he touch you anywhere?"

"Did he make use of his p*nis?"

"Did he do/use anything else to stimulate you?"

"What was your posture when he pierced you?"

That really disgusted me, and I stopped coming to church as a result.

8. ATTEMPTED SUICIDE AFTER THE INCIDENCE

It feels weird to be telling my story. I'm just sixteen years old, so I don't have a lifetime of experiences to draw on. It's also strange to know that this would be published for everybody to see. I've always kept my opinions to myself. Nobody knew about the internal strife; others saw me as cheerful and contented.

Being raped is a horrible event, especially for a fourteen-year-old who is already confused. After the rape, my brain shut off. I felt as though I were a shell, numb. All of my feelings were maintained, including agony, shame, rage, guilt, sadness, and confusion.

I had the sensation of being an outsider. I saw myself smiling, laughing, and enjoying myself, but I didn't feel any of it. I didn't recognize the face gazing back at me when I looked in the mirror. That's when I started cutting. It allowed me to feel

66

both my presence and pain, although of a different kind. I had some control over my chaotic existence because I was in control of a controlled suffering.

When my parents found out about the severance, they were shocked and bewildered. I refused to talk about it or tell them anything. I couldn't bring myself to discuss the rape. I'd feel it if I spoke about it, and it'd be real. I wanted to pretend it never happened, and it was easier to do so if no one knew.

They took me to a therapist I detested. I decided that visiting a therapist wasn't the solution and that the best option was to quit. If I left my city and went to a boarding school, I could get away from all of my problems. Naturally, that did not work. I couldn't get away from my problems because I couldn't get away from myself. When I realized this, I felt like I'd hit rock bottom. I'd visited a slew of therapists and social workers at this time. I wouldn't talk to any of them. I kept cutting and felt quite depressed. I was absent from school almost every day, and my grades plummeted as a consequence.

I couldn't get away from my problems because I couldn't get away from myself.

Then I started getting nightmares and vivid dreams about the encounter. I couldn't handle it any longer; I felt as if I was about to explode. I called a close friend I trusted one night and told her everything. She was quite kind and thrilled about it. She pressed me to inform my parents, but I was too scared. I was concerned about how people would react to me and treat me. What had happened had left me feeling ashamed. I was concerned that it was my responsibility, that I was to blame and would be held accountable.

I spent a lot of time chatting to my friend. I had so much bottled up inside me that when I opened up, it all gushed out at once. It was tough to deal with all of the emotions that were consuming me. I grew melancholy and stayed in bed a lot. Everything was simply too much. I had no ambition to achieve anything. I didn't shower, dress, or clean my room. I was really considering suicide. I worried as I considered the years ahead of me. I had no option but to commit; anything was better to the agony I was going through. I opted to tell my parents about the rape so they would understand when I died.

I spent a whole night writing my will, along with a suicide note and goodbye messages. I took the pills I'd stashed in my drawer, but I didn't swallow them. Instead, for some reason, I phoned a friend and told her of my plans. Even though it was late, after midnight, she drove right over. She sat up next to me, conversing and listening. She convinced me to put the pills away and go to bed. She promised not to tell anybody, but the next day she notified my parents. I was enraged at her. I knew she was acting in my best interests and how painful it must have been for her to betray me in that manner, but I despised her and resented myself for ever telling her anything.

My parents drove me to the hospital that night, where I was admitted to the psychiatric ward for immediate treatment. They diagnosed me with both post-traumatic stress disorder and severe depression. That was one of the worst nights of my life. I felt violated, as if I'd committed a horrific crime and was being punished for it. They removed everything from me, including my jewelry, iPod, phone, and clothes, forcing me to wear medical scrubs. Being there made me feel uncomfortable.

There were doctors, nurses, and physiologists everywhere. "What are you here for?" I was asked around fifty times a day. as well as "How are you feeling?" I'm not a straightforward person; I'm always going in circles. I disliked the straight questions and having to say things; if you didn't express your feelings, you had to stay longer.

It was also tough for me to be an observant Jew there. I had to wear pants, there was no kosher food, men and females were mixed, and I spent my whole childhood in an all-girls school. I wept the whole first day there. I soon became used to it. I even got used to the most inconvenient things, like not being allowed to use a fork or pencil and having to use the lavatory with a nurse. There were even some parts that I appreciated. I liked the group therapy the most; it was fantastic to talk to other kids who were going through similar things and could connect to you. I truly liked how safe I felt at the place. I was constantly frightened that someone was observing me at home.

After a week, I was released. After being so open and honest in the hospital, I felt more comfortable discussing what had happened. Once a week, I went to group therapy and met a physiologist who specialized in trauma. Things, though, were not improving. I was still depressed and suicidal. After I overdosed on medicine twice, my parents wanted to admit me back to the critical care unit. They referred me to a therapist, who prescribed antidepressants. I refused to take "happy pills," but she emphasized that they were there to help me when I was sad.

I recently disposed of all of my razors, medications, and unwanted stuff in a box.

I switched from the doctor to a therapist I liked and started to feel more connected to my group. I was able to communicate with them after opening up to them. They treated me as though I were a member of their extended family. I look forward to the group because it provides such an excellent chance to discuss difficulties and get assistance. I still have a lot of problems to work through.

My parents are often disappointed in me because I find it difficult to speak and be honest with them, but we both try to understand one other.

My friends have been wonderful. They have always been there to aid, love, and support me. My therapist is aiding me in putting the puzzle pieces of my life back together, healing my relationship with my parents, feeling good about myself, and working hard in school. I recently disposed of all of my razors, medications, and unwanted stuff in a box. It felt fantastic, and I felt strong.

I still get frightened when I look ahead, so I elevate my head and look down the long road.

I'm certain that I have a bright future ahead of me. Because if I can get through this, nothing will be able to stop me. Gd will be with me every step of the way. I have faith in Him; He will not let me down. I know God has put me through this because He also believes in me. He believes I am capable and capable of succeeding. I will not let Him down, and I will not let myself down.

I refuse to let this wickedness define who I am. The more I let this ruin my life, the worse it becomes. As a consequence, I composed this. To share my story in order for those who are going through similar situations to know they are not alone. I know the article I read gave me strength, and I hope it does the same for another girl. So, if you're reading this, my counsel is: Don't let people define you. You have the capacity to make judgments and to improve any situation. If I can do it, you can do it.

9. RAPED FIRST YEAR IN COLLEGE

Maya was raped by a buddy only a few weeks into her first year of college. Maya, like many survivors, did not recognize herself as a victim of sexual assault right away. She began processing her sexual assault episode six months later, after telling a friend about it.

"I was describing what had happened to me, but I hadn't spoken anything yet. 'He raped you,' said the person I was speaking with. When someone else brought it out to me and made it more real, that's when I started thinking about it. It was a huge shift in how I was processing my experience, and it became a little easier for me to talk about. I used to attempt to minimize it for myself by claiming that I had been 'taken advantage of.' But it has become necessary for me to call it what it was, rape."

Maya's months after the incident were hazy. The criminal harassed her on campus, making her feel insecure and unable to focus on her studies. She contacted an officer and secured a no-contact order, but owing to the university's crime reporting requirements, she was obliged to make a more formal report of the incident than she would have desired. When the offender discovered Maya had reported the rape, he concocted his own version of events, which Maya believes "made me seem crazy."

Maya had reviewed the university's criteria for reporting sexual assault and thought they were well-written at first, but issues emerged when the procedure was unexpectedly modified without her knowledge.

Maya does not want future survivors to be deterred from reporting sexual assault since the reporting procedure was tough for her. It was difficult, but she views it as an important step toward justice for herself and, maybe, other survivors.

As a consequence of the incident and the accompanying reporting process, Maya developed PTSD and anxiety. She went to counseling and found it helpful. She began blogging about her experiences and advocating for survivors of sexual assault as part of her rehabilitation process.

10. RAPED BY THE MAN I WAS DATING

I was raped by the man I was "dating". Yes, I am over 30 years old and I was raped. I trusted him and felt "secure" in his presence. He'd been unusually kind and attentive that night. We'd been together previously and it was usually a good time, until that night.

He was at a concert, and I went there for fun and to see him since it was a gorgeous full moon night. Because I knew he worked late, I informed him I was going and he escorted me to my vehicle. He instructed me to meet him in the rear. He went into my vehicle and raped me.

I said no, begged, kicked, wept. He claimed that it pleased him and remarked, "Well, I'm already in". I couldn't get away. I was shocked, afraid, and sad. How could he have done this to me? I've tried to figure out why, but I know I'll never get an answer.

I've been attempting to get my life in order. I'm not sure whether people actually want to know how I'm doing when they ask. Everyone thinks he's fantastic, a local military hero.

I did not report it. I felt as if I had nothing to lose. I believe in the healing power of sharing our experiences, and I believe in battling this messed-up society together. Even though I'm terrified, I don't want to remain mute.

11.I HAD TO MUCH DRINK AT A DORM PARTY

I had just relocated from Puerto Rico to Miami to begin my freshman year of college. It was two weeks into the semester and I was 17 when some friends asked me to a dorm party. I went, and my buddies quickly vanished. I began drinking as soon as I arrived, and I met this guy who was a junior there. We spoke all night and he kept bringing me drinks.

After a time, I asked him to my dorm room, which was only a few doors down. I just wanted to kiss him. I thought he was adorable. He suggested that we go to his house. I'm still not sure why I went. When we arrived, we began kissing, and he began stripping off my clothing, which I let. I didn't tell him "no" until he was within me.

I repeatedly urged him to stop, but he refused. I attempted to get away from him, but he grabbed my hands and forced them against the bed.

When he came to a halt, I requested him to take me home. I had no idea where I was and was terrified. He promised to take me home the following day.

The following day, I was covered with bruises. I was about to get out of the vehicle after he drove me home, and he told me that was how it was going to be, and he asked for my phone number. I'm still not sure why I handed it to him.

He phoned, and I was always hesitant to speak with him. He invited me out a few times, but I was terrified and always made up reasons. He eventually stopped phoning me and ignored me when he saw me on campus.

I had just told my closest friend I was a virgin at age twenty few days before the incident. It took me a long time to come to terms with the circumstances. I should not have left with him, and I should not have had so much alcohol, but I can't undo what occurred.

I haven't had sex with anybody else because I'm too terrified. I'm thinking of seeing the school counselor. I'm just trying to take each day as it comes.

12. I DID IT, I FELT ABUSED AT 13

I was 13. It's heartbreaking to think that at such a young age, someone can feel so violated. I had a lot of things going for me. I was the lead in a school play, had a 4.0 GPA, and was accepted into one of the greatest high schools in the state.

Still, given what had transpired, none of this made any sense to me. I was elected Drum Major for our Marching Band at our school. Steven, the assistant Drum Major, had always been lusty. We were great pals. We spoke on the phone virtually every day. I typically ignored his sexual comments. For a time, I thought they were amusing.

He came over to my home about a week before our TV debut at a parade. We were meant to discuss parade preparations, but we never did. Instead, he drew me into a poker game. We started undressing each other. It seemed like I was doing everything on my own. I was afraid to continue, but also afraid to quit. He eventually reached the point when he dropped the cards. He then directed me to perform oral sex on him. He departed after I had done him that favor. He returned, demanding it twice more. I did it both times because I was too terrified to stop or say no.

He never talked to me again after the third time. Ever. I felt betrayed. I felt like a slacker. He would periodically slip me a note or write me a letter in which he called me a whore, a slut, and a jerk. I didn't report it because I was afraid he'd twist the tale. After all, I'd done it three times before.

I eventually informed my closest friend, who was also Steven's closest friend. My buddy Matt questioned Steven about the situation. Steven flipped it around and said I asked him for it. Matt never talked to me the same way after that. He made me feel like a squatter.

I immediately went to Matt Hall, my lifelong best buddy (A different Matt). He persuaded me that it wasn't my fault and that I had been raped. He got it and was a Band-Aid for my wounds. He got it and was my shoulder to weep on. I admired him for it. I'm a few months older and a few months wiser now. Steven is still not talking to me. He still refers to me as a whore. But I'm aware that it's not my fault. I'm certain he'll receive what he deserves in the future. Despite my flaws, I know that some people adore me.

13. I WAS TWO YEARS OLDER, NO ONE WOULD HAVE BELIEVED ME

I'm not sure where to begin or what to say. Even today, it's difficult to speak about because I feel responsible. I believe it will always feel like my fault. It all started when my boyfriend dumped me. I was beyond myself, enraged, and horribly wounded. A few weeks later, he contacted me to continue the connection as "a strictly sexual relationship," and I agreed as a method of keeping him around.

A few months passed, and then one night when he arrived at the home, his buddy Greg was in the vehicle. I didn't think about it until we were on the highway, driving to an unknown destination. When I questioned where we were heading, they informed me I was supposed to have sex with one while performing oral sex on the other. I told them I didn't want to, and when we arrived at our destination, an abandoned campsite in the middle of the woods, they assured me I didn't have to. Greg walked into the vehicle as I had sex with my ex.

My ex then went inside the vehicle to chat with Greg as I stood outside in the rain dressed. He reappeared and informed me that if I didn't want to be left there, I could have sex with Greg. I had no idea what to do. I had no idea where I was or how to go home, and the journey had taken at least an hour, and we were at least a fifteen-minute drive from the closest phone, so I had sex with Greg. I informed my ex I would n't ever want to see him again the following day. Greg kept emailing me and telling me falsehoods, and I simply let him chat with me while I ignored him.

Greg and his buddy Joe asked me to Greg's place for a pool party a few weeks later. I didn't believe them, so I phoned their close friend Kristin, who confirmed everything. I went over there, and just Kristin, Greg, and Joe were present. Kristin fled as soon as I stepped into the pool. When I wanted to get out of the water, Greg and Joe had pushed me away from the ladder, to the other side of the pool, and while Joe held my feet, Greg untied the top of my bathing suit and tossed it out. Joe attempted to pull off the bottom of my swimming suit while I yelled and wailed, but I had gotten my feet free enough to kick him in the jaw.

Greg took me around the pool, then out, inside, and up to his room, where I was informed I couldn't go until I performed oral sex on him. I wept for a half-hour as he informed me that at that time, I could have had oral sex with him and walked home. I sobbed some more until I realized I couldn't go until I'd performed oral sex on him. Then he threw me out of his room, so I returned to the pool, changed into my swimming suit, and walked home. I quickly took a shower and washed my teeth.

I knew I couldn't go to the cops because Greg is two years younger than me — he's 16 and I'm 18 — and both he and Joe are much larger and stronger than me. Also, where I live still follows the old law of "if it's not genital-to-genital, it's not truly rape," so if it got out, they'd both twist it such that it was consensual and I'd face statutory rape charges. So far, I haven't informed anybody about what happened to me.

14. ONCE IS ENOUGH; IF I WERE THE JUDGE

I hope this helps someone. I'm not even sure where to begin. My uncle molested me when I was approximately 4 or 5 years old when I was spending the summer at my grandmother's home. It was hot, and I had been playing in her yard sprinkler, and he had been watching me.

He came into my room later that day, when my grandma and I were both taking midday naps. I didn't know he was with me until he pressed down on me. I recall the stench of booze, old cigarette smoke, and putrid perspiration. He yanked my pants down before I was fully awake and started fondling me. I remember being scared and whimpering, but he threatened to murder me and my baby brother if I made any noise or notified anybody. Something slashed my upper thigh, maybe his zipper or pocket knife. The scar is still there. I was scared. He said he could tell I wanted it by the way I was behaving earlier in the day. He raped me by pressing my face into the bed pillow.

I kept silent during it all, even for a time after he went. When I entered the restroom, I saw blood on my nightgown and on my legs. I cleaned it off, changed my panties, and climbed back into bed. I felt so insignificant and unhappy. My grandma sent me home a few days later because I was always sobbing and had a fever. I wish it had been the last time I was raped. I was so little at the time that my recollections are blurry around the edges. Unfortunately, my other recollections are vivid.

My self-esteem has never been very high. When I was 16, I became involved in an abusive relationship. In every manner conceivable, the guy abused and intimidated me. I was terrified of him, particularly of what he may do to me if I offended him. During our relationship, he raped and abused me and had other guys rape and assault me multiple times. He insulted and dismissed me. Rapes were simply one of many terrible techniques of torture he used.

I abandoned him by breaking up with him and fleeing the state. While I was in treatment, I lived with a family friend for a few years. I never filed any charges. I considered it but concluded that nothing could ever compensate for what he had done to me and that my life couldn't take any more interference, no matter how well-intentioned. Now that I think about it, I wish I had gone to the police. What I want most is to know that he will never do this to anybody else again. What he did to me is incomprehensible. He left scars on my body and harmed my spirit.

It feels really unjust that I am the one who suffers as a result of these rapes. In flashbacks and dreams, I relive the incidents. If I were a judge, I would make sure that the rapist suffers the emotional toll of rape, and that he relives the horror and suffering from the victim's perspective every time he sleeps or is disturbed. I would definitely make it such that the victim never had to experience her attack again. **Once is enough!**

15. I SURVIVED ABUSED BY MY FATHER, UNCLE AND A PREACHER; MY MOTHER COULD DO NOTHING

My abuse most likely started when I was approximately 6 or 7 months old. At the time, it was just me and my mum. We were then reunited with my father. (We were separated due to his employment.) I believe he was envious of the attention I received. It had been just my mother and I since I was born, and I wasn't 'in the way,' which had been the case throughout my childhood and maybe until my father's death a few years ago.

My gut sense is that I was sexually molested at this age as well. When I was around three years old, I was left alone and abandoned. I recall my dread, as well as anything else a child experiences at that age. I was obviously perplexed. It was a punishment for not finishing my food quickly enough for them.

Surprisingly, I did not eat well. My mother even brought me to the doctor to check if there was anything wrong with my throat. I'm curious why. I still have difficulty eating and swallowing, and I sometimes vomit when I recall what was rammed into my mouth that had no place being there!

When I was alone that night, I wondered, 'didn't they love me?' I was staring down on the bed, at me, this tiny bewildered, wounded young child, when I got memories of my father sexually assaulting me, and my mother looking at me. 'What were they up to with me?'

My father reprimanded me when I was approximately 4 or 5 years old by bringing me out into the dark night, placing my left hand in the front door, reaching in, locking the door, and slamming it shut on my hand. He bolted, as I remained there screaming. Only the tips of my fingers were trapped. But it did something

95

considerably more profound to my emotions. My mother eventually came to the door and let me in, never remarking on what had transpired.

I also have many...TOO MANY...memories of being beaten with the wire side of a wire, hair brush, belts, and branches from trees in our yard that I had to go get myself. If the branches weren't heavy enough, I'd have to go out and buy another one, or HE would. So I'd select the largest one I could find and climb down the tree. Then I had to wait and wait for him to come out and put it on my naked flesh.

I also recall the metallic end of the razor strap...and the sound it made. When he was using it on me, I recall his left hand holding my left hand to protect me from falling. Knowing he was going to use this on me, I was expecting a one or two week delay. (This all is VERY hard to write).

The beatings continued until I was 11 or 12 years old, when he began kissing me on the lips. It was a disgusting kiss that I despised and a demonstration of love that, deep down in my young girl heart, I needed yet despised because I knew it was phony. I eventually quit.

Since as early as I can remember, I've been told that I was unimportant, ugly, obese, and dumb in every manner possible. I was taught that it didn't matter what I thought or felt. I was told that I had no wants and no emotions worth paying attention to. I was told I was selfish, "stubborn, and crazy from the day I was born." I had to mask my pain when I was injured. I had to remain in the rear bedroom when I was unwell and couldn't come out. My mother would poke her head in the door at lunchtime and offer me a dish of food. She would not approach me. There is no consolation or affection. I felt disgusted and sick!

Then there were the occasions when I was smacked across the face and head, grabbed up and shaken, my head banging against the wall as my father shook me. Another of his favorites was slamming my brother's and mine heads together. I'd see the stars!

Then there were the marble-filled socks, which were kept for automobile rides. The sock would swing back at my head. All of this was done "because I love you." "It pains me more than you do." The ONLY time I was ever laid on my parent's lap was after my father had just beaten the hell out of me. He'd attempt to convince me that he did it because he loved me and I was such a jerk. (I was never held on my mother's lap.) I couldn't believe it. But I did think that I was awful.

My earliest vivid and clear recollection of sexual abuse, which I will never forget, happened when I was around 4 or 5 years old. I believe it began much earlier. BUT THIS I WILL NEVER FORGET. It lasted a long period, many years. I was being raped by a girl eight older than I was. It was terrible and never ended. I recall lying in her bed, stuck between her and the wall, while she raped me. I felt befuddled, imprisoned, DIRTY....and helpless.

When I was around 5-6 years old, I was abused by two other people.

My uncle raped me with a knife held to my neck when I was nine years old to keep me quiet. My four cousins were in the same room, and I believe they saw it. I believe they were also victims. One of them has subsequently committed suicide. I haven't felt strong enough to contact the others yet, but I will.

This cretinous scumbag of an uncle is still alive. Now I understand why I was always terrified of him and had a strange sensation around him as a child and even as an adult. As an adult, I only saw him once. He despised me and was furious that I was leaving the state!

Something terrible also occurred to me when I was approximately 7 or 8 years old. The memories are just now beginning to surface. I don't want to know, but I know I have to if I'm going to live and go on with my life. But that will be my childhood's last demise.

When I was 11, I was raped repeatedly by a preacher who threatened me with a pistol. This man, no, BEAST, also sodomized me. I was told it was my fault and that if I informed anybody, I would die. To tell the truth, it's been a pain. I was afraid for my life because I told. But I'm telling you RIGHT NOW. I've had several anxieties and thoughts that I deserved to die. I KNOW I DESERVE TO LIVE AND THRIVE, AND YOU DO TOO. This is not always simple to remember.

Except for the abuse I stated, I have no recollection of the years between the ages of 7 and 11. I have a strong feeling there was a lot more. When I was 11, my mother bathed me, evidently attempting to scrape off my skin, particularly my breast. I still despise her for crossing boundaries. Another minister crossed the line again when I was 17 years old.

I suppose I should state here that I am now battling to accept that all of this is genuine, that it occurred to me. "Are these fabricated memories?" I certainly don't want to confess that my own parents breached those lines. My mother, on the other hand, I recall setting me up for my father's physical, verbal, and mental abuse. There was no protection from anything else that transpired.

I recall wanting to run away, planning it, but knowing I'd be discovered, taken home, and beaten to within an inch of my life. I recall imagining that my parents had died, then cried and felt bad for doing so. I recall telling my mother about all the blood and her assuring me that 'it is nothing'.

I question myself now, if none of this truly occurred, if it is false memories, then why do I vomit violently, attempting to throw up the 'thing' that was jammed into my mouth? Why do I gag when I eat hard-cooked eggs? Why do I have no faith in anyone? Why do I know absolutely nothing about love? Why do relationships worry me so much? Why do I seek frequent reassurance from others that they really care about me and will not abandon me? Why is there depression? Why are there panic attacks? Why the heartbreaking anguish that makes me feel as if my heart will shatter in two, the pain (emotional) that causes me to moan in the night and sob deep within, with nary a tear flowing from my eyes? The list is endless.

What is the significance of my Post Traumatic Stress Disorder diagnosis? Why do I retreat into my shell at the first provocation? Why have I almost killed myself on many occasions? Why do I claw, tearing flesh, and creating bodily agony for the sake of 'it feels so good'? Do you believe I've been abused?

It's difficult to confess that my "ideal family" was far from perfect. And now, as I walk through the memories, they simply keep rushing at me, unbidden, unwelcome. My body also recalls vomiting, pelvic, pubic, and rectal agony, as well as bleeding. I wonder one more: was there abuse in my life?

Until recently, I thought of myself as a victim. I never believed I'd be able to call myself a survivor. I'm not sure when I began using that term to describe myself. But I am. WE ARE SUCCESSORS. We have survived the most heinous conflict, the fight for life. It is not finished, but the worst has passed and we have survived.

Is this something I always believe? I don't think so. Sometimes the agony is so excruciating that I feel this is the worst it can be and that it will never cease. But, in actuality, it will come to an end. The toughest part was living through it, which is why we shut it out. Our bodies became numb (and still do, as I recall), and we occasionally left our bodies behind, detaching ourselves from what was going on (I also do this as I remember). But we made it.

I now know that I was abused as a baby and that I was raped until I was 19 or 20 years old. This has been quite difficult to bear. It's quite difficult. But I take each day as it comes. I AM GOING TO HEAL!!!

16. SQUEEZING MY NIPPLES, HE FLIPPED ME ON MY STOMACH AND ANALLY RAPED ME

In 1995, I relocated from California to Texas with my partner. We broke up when we were living there because he didn't enjoy the commitment. I was working at a radio station and had a crush on Scott, who was also a coworker. While I was dating my boyfriend, he and I went out as friends, and I would tell him how things weren't going well. My boyfriend and I split up at the end of June, and I spent the Fourth of July with Scott and his pals in 1995. (Scott had just quit the station). We all got drunk and partied all night.

He'd kiss me and then claim he felt weird about it since I was like his younger sister. We got into his vehicle at the end of the night, and he started touching me. We all went back to his place, where he got into an altercation with another female over money. I walked into his bedroom because I didn't want to deal with it. We started kissing as soon as he walked in. He appealed to me. I was overjoyed that we were together! He left the room for a few moments and returned as someone else.

He'd been seeking ecstasy all night, but he'd never found it, as far as I knew. That's why he and the girl were arguing. When he returned, he lay on top of me in his underpants and we began playing about. I wanted to have sex with him. But as I removed my clothing, he began behaving strangely. He'd chuckle in a menacing tone - it seems foolish, but it's true.

While I shrieked and screamed, he flipped me on my stomach and anally raped me. He whacked my behind and left massive red handprints. He rolled me over again. I stopped screaming when he started having sex with me. WHY? I'm not sure. I just lay there. He wanted me to proclaim his name and how wonderful he was so that his housemates could hear. No, I didn't. When I attempted to get up, he pinched my arm (resulting in a horrible bruise) and then started squeezing my nipples (when I got home, I found that my nipples had bled). We went on like this for a long time...him shouting and laughing, me screaming and freezing.

I simply lay there after he was through. I either slept off or passed out. He was stroking my crotch and told me I was the greatest sex ever when I awoke. I immediately stood up and began to dress. He then called me a whore, a slut, and everything else he could think of. I returned home. Showered. And then did nothing. I hung up when he phoned the following day as if nothing had occurred.

"How was your 4th of July?" everyone would inquire. What do you think? I eventually informed a few people that I had been attacked, not raped. One pulled me kicking and screaming to the police station, where I screamed and blamed myself. He appealed to me. I wished I could be with him. It is my fault. The cops had to let it go since there was no proof and I hated myself.

I went through so many emotions and stages, including a particularly awful one in which I desired vengeance in the most heinous manner. I quickly left Texas and returned to California. After the rape, I had been sexual with others, but not with anybody I cared about. When I returned to California, I met David. He was the kindest guy I'd ever met. We married in June of 1996, after a quick relationship.

Sex was never an issue for us until we were married and discovered new depths in our love. I started to retreat and didn't want him to touch me. I was experiencing terrible spells of depression and had no idea why. When July 4th arrived in 1998, I sought out Scott and contacted him. He was overjoyed to hear from me! I informed him that he was a rapist and that I wished he perished in hell.

Then she hung up. That was such a thrill! But the depression worsened.

In September 1998, I finally saw a therapist, and the healing process started. Julie was fantastic! She specialized in rape therapy and made me feel less alone. I didn't want to have the conversation we had, but I knew I had to. She forced me to admit that, indeed, I had been raped. I didn't want anal sex even if I wanted to have sex with Scott. His slapping and twisting of my nipples were not appreciated.

I was more concerned with not fighting him off. I had taken self-defense classes! But she pointed out that Scott weighs over 200 pounds and trains out, and that while slapping and injuring me (125 pounds), I would not have survived if I had continued to fight. That jolted me awake. She could give me countless tales to fit everything I thought I was alone in. She forced me to confront the devil for me to take control.

I sent a letter to Scott explaining what had transpired. He now has a permanent reminder of what he did. I'm feeling considerably better, and my relationship with my spouse has improved. Of course, certain movies or news articles are off-limits to me. David and my mother are the two people I trust the most, yet I can't tell them everything. I wish to shield them... But I want to assist other ladies.

Nobody should be held responsible for their rape. They are not to blame! Yes, I loved Scott, but when things grew unusual and I shouted NO, it became rape. My one dream for closure would be to confront Scott in person. I understand that other survivors do not have the opportunity to submit a letter as I did, but I still want more.

True Rape Stories

CHAPTER FOUR

CONCLUSION

RAPE RECOVERY

Rape healing is a real possibility. It takes time and work to recover from rape, yet you may not only survive but also flourish thereafter.

If you've been raped, you're not alone, and you should know that rape does not mean the end of your health, sex life, or any other aspect of yourself.

Medical Care

This is the First Step in Rape Recovery. Medical care should be the primary step in your rape recovery strategy.

This procedure may check for sexually transmitted illnesses or infections, estimate pregnancy risk, and address any physical problems. It is important to seek medical attention as soon as possible to prevent worse difficulties in the future. Medical care professionals will usually recommend you to other providers who may assist you in recovering from rape.

Rape Rehabilitation

Rape healing may include a variety of activities, including formal therapy. Not everyone who has been raped feels the need for professional counseling, although it may frequently benefit and speed up the rehabilitation process. Formal therapy is especially crucial if the results of the rape are upsetting. These consequences might include:

- Remembering the incident of the rape
- Gain or loss of weight
- changes in eating or sleeping habits
- Feelings of guilt or responsibility
- Feeling uncontrollable
- Fear or anxiety that is unexplained
- Feeling down or hopeless?

- alterations in your thoughts regarding the opposite sex
- The fear of your partner
- Alterations in your sexual reactions (e.g., lack of desire, lack of orgasm, painful intercourse, etc.)

You want to speak to someone about the rape and/or your emotions.

Rape therapy is often used in the rape recovery treatment. This treatment may be given one-on-one or in a group setting. You and your spouse may also benefit from couple's therapy to deal with the rape's impact on your relationship.

COPING WITH SEXUAL ABUSE

Learning to care for yourself again after being raped is a big part of dealing with it. Rape survivors often feel unclean or guilty, and although these sentiments should never be felt, they are genuine and may hinder someone from taking proper care of themselves. Self-care is a vital aspect of rape rehabilitation.

Bodily self-care refers to taking care of your physical needs, which many people overlook.

Physical self-care comprises the following:

- Diet

While everyone forgets to eat correctly at times, it's important to take an effort to guarantee sufficient nourishment while recuperating from trauma. If your body feels well, your mind is more likely to follow suit.

- Exercise

Exercise may help alleviate stress, weariness, and depression. Even a short stroll in the middle of the day may be beneficial both psychologically and physically.

- Sleep

Many individuals are chronically sleeping deficient, which may lead to negative emotions. Most individuals need 7-10 hours of sleep every night to operate efficiently.

Getting over being raped entails taking care of oneself emotionally as well.

Emotional self-care involves the following:

- Counseling

Consulting with a therapist, counselor, or psychologist may aid in your recovery from rape.

- Journaling

For some individuals, writing down their thoughts and emotions in a journal is beneficial.

- Exercises in meditation or relaxation

HOW TO HELP A RAPE VICTIM

It's heartbreaking to see a loved one go through a horrible incident like rape, and you may be unsure how to assist a rape victim. It may be challenging to support a rape victim, but it is wonderful to know that you are supporting someone who has gone through something unspeakable. Both men and women may be raped, and both men and women can help the victim. Gender is unimportant here, but support is.

There are several things you may do to help a rape survivor. It all begins with your attitude to the victim. It is critical not to pass judgment on the rape victim and instead to listen to her and let her know you are there to support her. Remember that it takes time for a rape survivor to recover. Supporting a rape survivor entails not rushing them and accepting that they will recover in their own time.

There are additional things you can do to help a rape survivor:

- Respect your loved one's decisions and avoid pressing them to accomplish things for which they are not prepared.

- If the rape victim is contemplating suicide, get aid immediately and follow up with them regularly.

- Encourage the rape victim to report the incident, but remember that her choice is final.

- Encourage the rape victim to seek professional assistance if necessary.

- Go attend medical or legal appointments with the rape victim

Remember that when you're helping a rape victim, you need also take care of yourself. You can't assist anybody else if you're not healthy. You may also need professional rape assistance for yourself.

DATING A RAPE SURVIVOR

While dating a rape survivor might be intimidating, keep in mind that someone is sexually attacked every two minutes in the United States. You will most likely date a rape survivor if you haven't already.

Dating a rape survivor may elicit a range of emotions in both you and your partner. You may be indignant about the rape, overprotective of the victim, and seeking revenge on the rapist. These are typical sentiments that should be shared with your spouse or a professional.

It's important to recognize that, although you may believe your support is insufficient, the rape victim appreciates it even if she can't always show it.

Keep the following in mind while dating a rape victim:

- For a while, the victim may lose interest in sex or certain sexual behaviors. This is natural and does not constitute a rejection of you.

- Due to unanticipated sensations of dread or anxiety, your partner may need to abruptly end sexual contact. Respect that choice and quickly discontinue communication. Again, this is not about you; it is about the rape.

You may also lose interest in sex for a while as a result of the rape. You could think the sufferer is "filthy" or "infected." This is completely natural and should be addressed with a medical practitioner.

In brief, rape may have a tremendous impact on both you and your spouse, but it is possible to work through those emotions with open lines of communication and potentially the assistance of a professional.

Made in the USA
Monee, IL
09 August 2023

40754831R00069